B.C.

BT 993.2 .S455 1982
Seilhamer, Frank H.
  Adventure in faith : the Apostles' Creed
and us /

Adventure in Faith

DR. FRANK H. SEILHAMER

Adventure in Faith

THE APOSTLES' CREED AND US

NEW WORLD PRESS • YORK, PENNSYLVANIA
1982

BT
993.2
.S455
1982

© DR. FRANK H. SEILHAMER • *August, 1982*

*To the members of Advent Lutheran Church,
York, Pennsylvania, my partners in a
ministry of love and trust.*

Introduction

This is a time when the whole world seems to be coming apart. Moral absolutes have been shattered, the long-trusted economic security that followed the Great Depression has been shaken around the world, a nuclear holocaust appears to be forming on the horizon of the future, and in the midst of it all people are searching for ground on which they can stand with some degree of certainty. What holds fast anymore? On what can we depend? Is anything from the past reliable, *really reliable* now . . . even the *God* of Abraham, Isaac, Jacob and our forebearers? We all long for something, some One in whom to believe. Where can that anchor for existence be found?

This little book is an attempt to look life, with all of its perplexities and opportunities, full in the face and "watch to see what God will say to (us)" (Habakkuk 2:1) about it. Using the *Apostles' Creed,* that summary of the Christian Church's faith in that God whose world, with all its puzzlements it is, as our road map, we will be off on an adventure in faith to see what we can learn about living in these times. With the wisdom and inspiration the Creed has embedded in it I am convinced that the trek can be a moving and strengthening journey.

FRANK H. SEILHAMER

Pentecost 1982

Apostles' Creed

I believe in God, the Father almighty,
    creator of heaven and earth.

I believe in Jesus Christ, his only Son, our Lord.
    He was conceived by the power of the Holy Spirit
        and born of the virgin Mary.
    He suffered under Pontius Pilate,
        was crucified, died, and was buried.
    He descended into hell.
    On the third day he rose again.
    He ascended into heaven,
        and is seated at the right hand of the Father.
    He will come again to judge the living and the dead.

I believe in the Holy Spirit,
    the holy catholic Church,
    the communion of saints,
    the forgiveness of sins,
    the resurrection of the body,
    and the life everlasting. Amen.

Contents

Adventure in Faith

APOSTLES' CREED I

I Believe

Several years ago there was a popular radio program entitled, *"This I Believe."* It featured famous people from various fields who told of the convictions and principles that governed their lives. Although there was as wide an assortment of beliefs as there were guests, each one had a *definite set of convictions* that served as guideposts for their existence.

Whether we know it or not *all people* have such reference points of faith embedded in their hearts. The word we translate *Creed* comes from the Latin *"Credo,"* which means "I believe," and every person who ever drew breath "believes" in something or other. Even though we may never put them into words or write them down, these basic assumptions are present, and like unseen sextants they set our course toward shaping what we are and dream of being.

In the *Apostles' Creed* the Christian Church has such a guide by which it travels. Though summed up in just over 100 words, it has piloted our course for many centuries. To understand it and its role we must understand at least two things about it . . .

> *First*   —the Apostles' Creed is like a *diary* that records the church's past experience;
>
> *Secondly*—it is like a *road map* whose purpose it is to guide future explorers in their venture in faith.

Like a diary, the Creed is the account of the religious experience of Christians who lived with God through the centuries. It tells of what they learned about him as they walked through good days and bad, thick and thin, with him at their shoulder. Like any personal log it was a growing thing. It took what was reported by millions of Pilgrims and boiled it down into the powerful and concentrated declaration we have today.

Although we call it the *Apostles'* Creed, it was not written by those first 12 leaders Jesus hand-picked to follow him. In fact, it did not begin to take written form until the early second century A.D. and arrive in the form we now know it until the 8th century—long after the Apostles were dead. But it carries their name because it declares the faith by which these friends of Jesus lived, taught and died. It was, in a sense, their Spiritual journal to which others who followed them added detail as they too lived and learned, putting their common experience into capsule form.

The early followers of Jesus were Jews. As part of that people they had already come to believe in a God who was One, and dealt with them as a loving Father, in contrast to their pagan neighbors. To express that faith, they produced the oldest creed we have in our heritage, found in the sixth chapter of Deuteronomy:

> "Hear O Israel, the Lord our God is One Lord, and you shall love the Lord your God with all your heart, and with all your soul, and with all your might." (DEUTERONOMY 6:4–5)

That faith was enough until they came into contact with Jesus—a meeting that forced another entry into their diary of religious experience. At first they met and saw him as a man—a good man—a great leader and lover of people—a healer, but just a *man*. But the day came when they saw that Jesus was *more* than *that!* He was *God* who had taken the form of a human being to draw close and touch them. And from the mouth of Simon Peter, by the river at Caesarea Philippi, came the words that were to form the *second article* of the Creed:

"Thou art the Christ, the son of the living God." (MATTHEW 16:16)

In the days after Jesus' death and resurrection the groundwork for the *third article* of the Creed was laid. He had promised them a Divine Comforter to lead and support them when he would have to leave them. When he ascended, a power moving like "a mighty rushing wind," blew among them as God wrapped his arms around them in a new way. Never again were they to be alone—or feel abandoned. And to explain what it was that had happened, they declared after that presence of God had swept over them:

"We believe in the Holy Spirit."

It was not a new God they had met, mind you, but another dimension of God that had hovered over the world at creation.

So vital was all of this that they had experienced, that they wanted to give it expression and share it with any who would listen. They wrote it down and compressed their diary into the forerunner of the Creed we have today. Over the centuries, as need arose, the Church made its statement more explicit and detailed, but the *basic content* of it never changed as more and fuller declarations about the God who was alive and near were set down. It was never assumed that in their Credo the Church had God neatly tied up and packaged. But it was a *sketch* of what God had shown about himself. And because it was that they couldn't keep it for themselves, but ran through the world with it ringing from their lips.

They used it in every possible way. They *recited it* when they gathered for Communion—not to remind God who he is but to speak about him to inquirers and one another.

They *chanted* it at baptisms and funerals, talking about the God who meets us at *each end of life!*

They used it to *instruct new members* in the church, giving them the faith in a nutshell.

They *professed* it before tormentors, using it often as a prayer that ushered them into the arms of the God who had made them.

In every *way*, and in *everything*, this personal diary of their belief was kept open and in the forefront of their lives. It was their *will* and *gift* to the church who would follow about who it was on whom their faith was built. It was as Saint John was to declare:

> "That which was from the beginning, which we have heard, which we have seen with our eyes, which we have looked upon and touched concerning the word of life. . . . we proclaim also to you, so that you may have fellowship with us; and our fellowship is with the Father and with his Son Jesus Christ. And we are writing this that (your) joy may be complete." (I JOHN 1:1-3b-4)

And yet the Creed is more than a *diary* of a *past age*. If that was all it was it would be of value only to historians. The *Creed* still has a vital use for us as a *road map* to help us in our religious explorations, now and tomorrow.

As with any map, one of its uses is to help us benefit from the journeys of others. Like any map it tells us where others have looked over the landscape and found certain routes that lead to new and clear horizons. Their own treks have gotten them to their destinations and back again safely to give *us directions!*

The *Creed* is like that for you and me. It is not a roadblock that says, "Thus Far and no Farther. This is *all* there is to God, and all you *may* or *can say* about him!" It is not intended to put a *limit* on our explorations in the faith. It is not like an iron mold into which all minds are to be poured, being *restrictive* and *squeezing* and *confining*. Some people have opposed creeds because they have feared them as prisons or chains on the spirit and inquiry!

It is not that! But it can help keep us from the pitfalls and dead-ends others have found in their journeys of faith. The very brevity and spareness of the Creed gives us room to write in its margin many of our own personal notes of what *we* learn about God in the living of *our* days.

On any trip, not all eyes will see all the same things on the landscape. Each will glimpse something another has missed or dis-
missed. But when at journey's end notes are compared, more of the
whole picture can be reconstructed.

The *Apostles' Creed* is like that. It is not the work of one hand or one
head or one heart or one generation. It is the treasury that has been
gathered from uncounted numbers of men and women of God,
sensitive, thoughtful, honest travelers who have turned to tell us:

"This is a good road!
 It has the clearest insights into the God who travels it and
 stands at its end."

We can ignore it—of course we can—and go it alone. At *best,* we
usually will find ourselves traveling and struggling over territory
that could have been made easier and more exciting with a little
help. At *worst,* we can end up lost in a maze, sidetracked by others as
impaired as we, a long way from the destination we had in mind
and spiritually befuddled!

Like any map, the Creed is almost useless *unless it is traveled.* You
never get the real thrills it has to offer sitting in a spiritual armchair
looking it over or repeating it. It is intended to move us to get up
and follow the leading of God who has prompted us to read it or
say it or to listen to its words in the first place and then *walk* with
him—and in the walk get to *know him* about whom the *Creed* sings.

To have that happen, start on the exploration with *however much
faith you have.* As you go, you will find that what Jesus said about
faith will be true. It is like a mustard seed, so small that it looks like
a grain of pepper, but which when put to work and planted, grows
into trees higher than a house.

Go as far as you can. Never be satisfied until you have reached the
final answers to the questions about life and God. When tests of
your faith arise as you live, don't accept easy and shallow answers
from *anybody,* and don't be afraid of pressing your faith! What is

true will stand fast when the testing is over. What *crumbles* was never worth holding onto in the first place.

Stick to your journey when the going gets tough. When contradictions and uncertainty hit you, *keep digging* and *climbing!* Note that Jesus never demanded full-blown faith from those who came to him. He simply said:

> "Come—follow—lean on me!
> Come, troubles and puzzlements and all."

In the last analysis that is all he will ask of any of us. His beckoning hand is waving us on to get up and go with him, having our minds and hearts filled along the way.

This is where the Creed points us . . . down the road with the Lord in an *adventure in faith*. Come with me and when we get back I suspect we will find new thrills every time we stand to declare . . . "I *believe* in God . . ."

I Believe in God The Father

"In the beginning God created the heavens and the earth. The earth was without form and void, and darkness was upon the face of the deep; and the Spirit of God was moving over the face of the waters. And God said, 'Let there be light'; and there was light. And God saw that the light was good; and God separated the light from the darkness. God called the light Day, and the darkness he called Night. And there was evening and there was morning, one day." (GENESIS 1:1-5)

"In the beginning God created the heavens and the earth," so goes the very first sentence on the very first page of the Bible. Though coming from the hand of a Hebrew who lived and died without ever giving us his name, the message and truth of which he had hold has outlived him and the billions of people who read and have believed what he had to say.

Wherever people have existed, regardless of their spot in history or place on the globe, each has struggled with that most basic of questions—*"How did I get to be?"* Looking for clues from all that has surrounded them, the overwhelming majority across the ages have been convinced that somehow an Almighty Being was the source of it all.

So convinced has been the Christian Church that such is the case that when it finally got around to writing its Creed, it embedded that affirmation right at the start of its profession of faith. There it stands today, as bold as can be, the forthright statement—

"I believe in *God* the Father Almighty, creator of heaven and earth."

Essentially that first Article of the Apostles' Creed makes two basic statements about God and his relationship to all that exists.

Right at the top it declares that every atom that was brought into being to make the universe blossom, leaped into life *from the hand* and *at the will of* God. Whatever it was, and however it took shape, its starting point was in the Almighty and still remains his possession. As the writer of the 24th Psalm said it—

"The Earth is the *Lord's* and the fullness thereof
The world and they that dwell therein.
For *he* has founded it upon the seas and established
it upon the rivers." (PSALM 24:1)

The heart of the matter is that God, like a Master Artist, fashioned this intricate system of life that envelopes us with no power other than his own. And when he set it in action he marked his product with a stamp that bears his coat of arms. Wherever you look, if you look closely enough, you can see the evidence of his hands having touched all of creation. He purposely left enough of his finger prints behind to serve as reminders of his presence for people such as we.

Nature, for instance, is like an open book telling us that God has been here. It is a treasury of wonders that lavishly illustrates a divine plan and organization, an intricate inter-relationship and balance so awesome that it has outstripped the ability of our combined minds to appreciate and explain them.

The vastness of it all, with heavens stretched above us spangled with trillions upon trillions of stars populating it from one horizon to the other, at the same time thrills me almost into ecstasy and stuns me into silence as I have looked at it through telescopes and from the flat of my back in the desert in Palestine. There, where there is no pollution to dull their radiance, the stars glitter like fireflies and the Milky Way looks like a bridge of sparkling talcum powder arched over the sky. They look so close you think you can reach up and catch them, and you see past them to sense the magnificent depth of space. The effect is breathtaking, literally breathtaking—so much so that when I have been there time seemed to stop as the chills went up my spine.

And I am not the only one who has been awed and dwarfed by that one facet of creation. The world famous astronomer, Sir James Jeans, has been struck by the same wonder over a lifetime of work. He tells us about it in the introduction of his book, *The Mysterious Universe,* where he writes:

> "The total number of stars in the universe is probably something like the total number of grains of sand on all the seashores of the world. . . . This vast multitude of stars are wandering about in space. . . . they travel through a universe so spacious that it is an event of almost unimaginable rarity for a star to come anywhere near to another star. For the most part each voyages in splendid isolation like a ship on an empty ocean."

What else, but an Almighty God, could have *imagined,* let alone created, a vastness and precision of such dimensions? Could it really have been *chance?*

Or turn your eyes and look *down* instead of *up* for clues to our existence. Put your eye to a microscope and focus on a droplet of water taken from a gutter, and view the miracle of God's *compression.* A speck dropped on a slide from the end of a pin and yet it is teeming with life in magnificent variety. Added to the *eye* that is itself taking in the wonder, the *brain* that is struggling to comprehend it, and the *body that encases both,* it staggers me to understand how anyone can resist saying with the Psalmist—

"Such knowledge is too wonderful for me; it is high,
I cannot attain it." (PSALM 139:6)

For on all of these facets of creation God has left his fingerprints. He purposely put "tongues in trees, books in brooks and sermons in stones" so that one dimension of life after another, like a syncopated choir, would sing out—

"Behind us stands God!"

For God has shot through even the most ordinary chunks of existence with signs of his presence so that as we look at, or bump up against it, we can glimpse the power as well as the extravagant goodness of God that has made *it* and *us* possible! For. . . .

"Is it not by his superfluousness (that) we know our God?

For to equal a need is natural, animal, mineral: but to fling rainbows over the rain and beauty above the moon

And secret rainbows on the domes of deep-sea shells, And make the necessary embrace of breeding beautiful also as fire:

Not even the weeds to multiply without blossom nor the birds without music:

There is the great humaneness at the heart of things, the extravagant kindness, the *fountain humanity can understand.* . . ."[1]

None of creation is a senseless shower of a playful magician. It is a signpost that has its finger pointing toward God. He who made the heavens crafted them to declare his glory—and when he pounded out the firmament his intention was to show his handiwork!

The second thing we say about God when we declare this first article of the Creed is that the awesome One, who worked it into being, is like a patient observant *Father,* who continually watches over and stays involved with what he made. He is no absentee landlord—no watchmaker who set the piece to running, then left it to tick unattended or sold it off and forgot it! He is so close to the affairs of life that, if we are sensitive to it, we can feel his breath!

[1] R. Jeffers, "The Excesses of God," *Be Angry at the Sun.*

Not only does he keep some things constant—like the balance that keeps the planets in their courses and the seasons following each other around the earth, but that same constancy reaches down to be involved in "minutia," like keeping your and my heart beating, gravity holding our feet to the earth, and seeing to it that the basic ingredients that make life on this speck of celestial real estate possible are here for us to use for *everyone's* benefit, if only we will.

In ways that most of us will never fathom, God is inextricably bound up in our lives, even during those moments or phases of life when we are oblivious to that fact, or convinced that we have been abandoned. Even when existence seems to have soured—and the bottom fallen out for us—the same God who before time existed willed that we should be here, is busy slipping his hand into our days, helping us to hold things together until the greater blessings he has in store for us have the time to arrive!

It may well have been to people who were having doubts about that being so that Jesus was speaking when he told his audience—

> "Look at the birds of the air—they neither sow nor reap nor gather into barns, and yet your heavenly Father feeds them. Are you not of more value than they?" (MATTHEW 6:26)

Aware that every one of our senses repeatedly gets dull to that involvement of God with us, Luther used his explanation of the first Article of the Creed as a kind of prod to tweek both our minds and hearts. Gently tapping us, he pointed us to that Creator's incessant activity as it worked itself out in his life and ours—

> "I believe," wrote the good doctor, "that God has made me and all creatures; that he has given me my body and soul, eyes, ears, and all my members, my reason and all my senses and still preserves them; also clothing and shoes, meat and drink and home, wife and children, fields, cattle and all my goods; that He richly and daily provides me with all that I need (note—not *want*) to support this body and life; that he defends me against all danger, and guards and protects me from all evil; and *all this* purely out of fatherly, divine goodness and mercy, without any merit or worthiness in me."

25

The emphasis on God's unending work on creation *now* and *here*, for *you* and *me*, is what is kept front and center. For that is where *it* and *he* always must be if God is to have *meaning* for the individual believer. The first Article of the Creed is just so many *words* if we cannot *see* and *feel* God at work in our lives. And to be able to *acknowledge* a God who does just that is not an easy thing in an age and land like our own.

Dr. George Daugherty, who succeeded Peter Marshall as the pastor at New York Avenue Presbyterian Church in Washington, tells about a Scottish preacher who came as guest speaker to his congregation, and who when finished with his engagement was taken by Daugherty on a week-long tour of the southeastern United States. Wanting to show off his country at her best, Daugherty took his friend to all the places where he could see the progress and technology that are America. It was to Bethesda Medical Center, then housing areas of Georgetown and Alexandria, and then to what was then Cape Canaveral, from which our first manned space shots had been launched. They finally landed back in Washington and ended with a luncheon in the dining room of the U.S. Senate. As they got ready to leave for the airport Daugherty said the man turned to him and asked, "Tell me, how does a preacher like you say to the people of America—You cannot save yourself?"

He had put his finger on one of our most tender and vulnerable spots! How hard it is, indeed, to get people like us to face up to the truth that we are not self sufficient and that God is involved in our destinies! What makes it so difficult to own up to is that almost everywhere you look what you see are things that seem to be built solely with our skills. Cities of steel and concrete and plastics sprawl in an almost unbroken string from Maine to Florida. Fly over it by night and you are never out of sight of lights on the ground. Rockets and space shuttles and space stations fly between us and the stars that used to astound us. Granaries are bursting, even in economic times as tough as these, showing that we have produced food enough not only to eat but to let rot! And all of it is the result of technology that can give one the sense of independence and invulnerability. They can produce an enormous tug within us to fix our gaze on our own hands and recite to the world and ourselves, not the first article of the *Apostles' Creed*, but of another one that begins—

"I believe that *these* have made us what we are."

That has been a deadly temptation God has had to contend with through the ages. One of the most trying times was at the moment when he had the people of Israel, not long out of Egyptian bondage, ready to enter the Promised Land. Although he had freed them from the shackles of a nation whose power was astronomical compared to theirs, though he had parted a sea to put safety between them and those who wanted to annihilate them, and despite the fact that he had fed them in a wilderness with meat and manna where food was so scarce that vultures circled waiting for them to starve—God knew that once the Israelites settled down in security his hour-by-hour involvement in their lives could be forgotten in a flash.

To keep them from the delusion that could lead to their destruction, God took the people aside for a word of warning. With Moses as his spokesman, he gave the people the words intended to keep them whole:

> "The Lord your God is bringing you into a good land, a land of brooks of water, of fountains and springs . . . a land of wheat and barley, of vines and fig trees and pomegranates, a land of olive trees and honey, a land where you will eat bread without scarcity, in which you will lack nothing, a land whose stones are iron, and out of whose hills you can dig copper. And you shall eat and be full. . . . Take heed . . . lest when you have eaten and are full, and have built goodly houses and live in them . . . and your silver and gold is multiplied, and all that you have is multiplied . . . beware lest you say in your heart 'My power and the might of my hand have gotten me this'. . . . I solemnly warn you this day that you shall surely perish." (DEUTERONOMY 8:7-10a, 17, 19b)

It is days like *that—good* days—that are our greatest threats to obliterating God from our consciousness! When life is *coming apart*, we look for him and run to him like puppies to a bone—

but—when life is on the rise,
　　when our careers are in their bloom,
　　when our dreams are being fulfilled,
　　when our groceries are secure,
　　and our health is vibrant and robust—

then it is that the Giver of the potential to receive these gifts is in danger of being *far out of our minds*. Rather strange, isn't it, that his own *generosity* gives God his greatest pain and problems with us!

In what I think is one of his most awesome gifts, God continues to hang in with us, holding us together while he waits for us to come to our senses. *Longing,* I think, for what every *lover* wants from the one to whom his heart is given—a sign that we *love him back*—and want him for our own. Sometimes, it seems, God is our divine wallflower. He stands in the shadows, the Giver of the banquet of life, waiting to be invited in by his guests! All it takes to set his heart to racing is for us to turn in his direction, and in the presence of all who are gathered around us, introduce him to all the world to see as the one we are proud to name—

"Our Father and Lord!"

I Believe in Jesus Christ

"Now while the Pharisees were gathered together, Jesus asked them a question, saying, 'What do you think of the Christ? Whose son is he?' They said to him, 'The son of David.' He said to them, 'How is it then that David, inspired by the Spirit, calls him Lord, saying, 'The Lord said to my Lord, sit at my right hand till I put thy enemies under thy feet?' 'If David thus calls him Lord, how is he his son?' And no one was able to answer him a word, nor from that day did any one dare to ask him any more questions." (MATTHEW 22:41–46)

"What do you think of the Christ?" is a question that has been asked of billions of people over the last twenty centuries. Though the query made its debut in Galilee one afternoon when Jesus threw it out to a group of Pharisees, the answering of it has been one of the most crucial issues of life for those who have had it put to them. Every person who has come up against the Carpenter from Nazareth has had to make up his or her mind about him.

Not everyone who has encountered Jesus has had the same estimate of him. Even while he was alive and preaching, the Galilean was a highly controversial figure. Wherever he went he caused a ruckus among the people who came to hear him. As they listened to what he had to say and watched his amazing works, some folks were drawn to *believe in* and *adore* him, while others went off *to snarl for his death*.

Jesus recognized and accepted that fact about himself:

> "Do not think that I have come to bring peace on earth," he said. "I have come not to bring peace, but a sword. For I have come to set a man against his father and a daughter against her mother." (MATTHEW 10:34–35)

That observation, made mid-way in his ministry, was prophetic as well as perceptive. Humanity in general has tended to divide itself into several camps where *who* and *what* he is are concerned.

One group has looked at Jesus and seen a *man* who was a *dreamer* and a *fool*. He was a mere human being whose imagination ran away with him. Not only was he afflicted with the *ordinary* delusions of grandeur, but he went so far as to identify himself with *God!* Basically he was no more than a country bumpkin nursing a warped mentality. As a religious fanatic making absurd claims, he finally met his due when the religious and secular authorities converged to silence his babblings with nails and a spear!

In the middle of the road have gathered those who have drawn a more tempered portrait of him. They ascribe to Jesus no fevered brain, nor are they willing to label him a quack. They have understood him to be nothing less than a *true prophet* sent from God. In the great tradition of such holy men, Jesus had a message to deliver. The teachings he proclaimed are noble guides to a good and abundant life. His insights added depth and helped make sense of living. But he was *not in any way more than a man*, they are quick to remind us. But he may well have been the *purest* and *greatest* man who ever drew breath.

The Christian Church is the third main body that has taken a stand on who and what Jesus is. Though within its ranks there are variations in viewpoints, two central truths about him stand at the heart of our faith. The Carpenter from Galilee is unlike any other Person who ever lived. At one and the same time, he is both *human* and *divine*. How this can be true we have never been able to explain fully. That it *is true,* nevertheless, we fervently declare in the second article of the Apostles' Creed:

"I believe in Jesus Christ, (God's) only Son, our Lord.
He was conceived by the power of the Holy Spirit
and born of the virgin Mary.
He suffered under Pontius Pilate,
was crucified, died, and was buried.
He descended into hell.
On the third day he rose again.
He ascended into heaven,
and is seated at the right hand of the Father.
He will come again to judge the living and the dead."

As with the Scriptures, the Creed goes to great pains to declare that Jesus was a *human being!* It marshalls all of its evidence of that fact and sets it out in unmistakable terms.

It begins with the simple but profound observation that Jesus was "born of the virgin Mary." That is, like any other child he had a mother, and he came into the world at the expense of her pains. Unlike the heavenly beings of Greek mythology, Jesus did not enter the world full-blown. On arrival he was a cuddly bundle whose hunger Mary erased when she nursed him and whose wet and drooping diapers she had to change! A startling affirmation it is when you get to taking it seriously, to realize that this God who came down to earth entered it without teeth!

As Jesus grew he went through the same routine as other children. He had to be taught to speak! After awhile when he could leave her lap, Mary watched as he crawled about on the dirt floor of their home. Eventually he was able to toddle and then walk with surer steps. From there he was off to run and play with other youngsters of his village and romp over the Judean hills.

When he came of age, he was sent to school to learn to read and write. Then taken in hand by the head of his household, he was taught a trade for a livelihood. As with any other carpenter, the young man Jesus spent his time fashioning ox yokes and furniture. And *his* hands got as calloused and splinter-ridden as the hands of any other of his trade.

And not only did Jesus go through the natural stages of physical growth as we do; he was intensely human when it came to the basic needs and emotions that mark us all. Like any other human being, he had to eat and drink and have time to rest from his labors. Just like us, he craved and enjoyed the companionship and closeness of other people. Note how seldom we meet him anywhere in the Bible where he is *alone!* More often than not, he is surrounded by crowds, or at least, a few of his friends.

His true humanity also showed through in his moments of pleasure and pain. He, above all, knew how to "rejoice with those who rejoice and weep with those who weep." He enjoyed celebrations and even performed his first miracle at a *wedding* so as not to end the festivities!

He was a man who was strong enough to be tender. He was able to cry on occasion when bruised by loss or disappointment. So he wept as he stood beside the tomb of Lazarus, a friend who died before he could reach him, as he did when he was met with the hard-headedness of the people in Jerusalem who would not accept him for what he truly was.

Yet nowhere was his humanity as much in evidence as during his last night and day on earth. In the Garden at Gethsemane, he sweated in agony, hoping Good Friday could be avoided. He was no "sicky" going around looking for crosses onto which he could climb! And when he was hung up on the top of Calvary he cried out in pain. And there, spiked fast where all could watch, he gave the final evidence to the world that he was a man among men by *dying* and going through that supremely human act of being sealed in a tomb, as it will be done one day for each of us! Whatever else he was, this much should be evident for all to see: in every way, Christ was made of the same stuff and fiber as we.

But the Apostles' Creed does not *end* with the declaration that Jesus was a *man!* It declares that he was something *we can never be*—he was also *divine*. He was not 50% human and 50% divine, which would have made him *neither man nor God*. But he was 100% of both, fully human and fully God—a mathematical problem that boggles our brains enough to force us to look at him with *new eyes,* and see him as he *really* is.

Intertwined with the phrases that bear witness to Jesus' humanity, the Creed has testimony swearing to the truth that Christ was someone who was "from out of this world:"

> "He was conceived by the power of the Holy Spirit . . .
> On the third day he rose again
> He ascended into heaven, and is seated at the right
> hand of the Father.
> He will come again to judge the living and the dead."

These things can't be said of anyone who lived before or after Jesus. They have their beginning and their end in him alone!

"Conceived by the power of the Holy Spirit" . . . is the Creed's way of reminding us that Jesus was *always God*. It's a simpler way of phrasing what the Gospel of John had to say in its opening paragraphs:

> "In the beginning was the Word, and the Word was with God, and the Word was God. He was in the beginning with God; all things were made through him and without him was not anything made that was made . . . and the word became flesh and dwelt among us, full of grace and truth; we have beheld his glory, glory as of the only Son from the Father." (JOHN 1:1–3, 14)

Jesus was not a human being who earned the right to become God's Son. *Before* he came to earth, he *already* was the *King of Heaven*.

"On the third day he rose again," is the declaration that not even death could hold him. When others are put into a grave and the earth is pushed into place *that* always seems *final*. But when Jesus was taken from the cross and entombed, and a huge stone was rolled against the entrance and sealed into place, *that* was *not final!*

When the friends of Jesus got to his grave on Easter morning, with no purpose in mind other than the final embalming of his *corpse,* they got the surprise of their lives. Waiting for them was not a dead Teacher but an angel with the message:

> ". . . you seek Jesus of Nazareth who was crucified. He has *risen,* he is not here; see the place where they laid him. But go, tell his disciples and Peter that he is going before you into Galilee; there you will see him as he told you." (MARK 16:6–7)

You see, out of the darkness of death Jesus had stepped alive and in full strength. With a power reserved for *God* alone, he had torn the lid from death's casket.

That he "ascended into heaven," took a place on God's "right hand" and "will come again," is another way of saying that the God-Man is still as *alive* and *in command* of things as he ever was! He who "from heaven to earth came down" reclaimed the throne he left to slip into our world in a cow stall. Now he stands, biding his time to return to gather up and take us home to spend eternity with him.

Only a *total fool* would claim these things for a mere man. But the Church from her birth until now has proclaimed that all of this is true about Jesus. She has based her very life on the fact that what she believes is true! That in actual fact our Lord and Master is both *true God* and *true man,* the one who died and yet is alive and with us *here, today!!!*

It is not, mind you, that the Church has been foolish enough to think that she could explain all of the "hows" and "wherefores" that surround the person of this God-Man. We freely admit that there are, and always will be, numerous questions that will remain unanswered about him. With minds as limited as our own, we cannot fully plumb the depths of the mysteries of God. What we must do is try with all that is in us to learn all we can of him—then pick up and follow him with what it is we know.

The wonderful thing about Jesus is that that is all that he asks us to do. He makes no more demands on us than he did on Simon Peter the morning he took that disciple aside for a walk on the beach by the Lake of Galilee. Their final breakfast together ended, the time was coming when Jesus was going to leave the disciples who had been his constant companions from the beginning of his ministry. Though they would feel his presence and he would leave them signs of his closeness, they would not *see* him again until the day when he would call an end to history. With Good Friday and the miracle of Easter behind them, Jesus wanted to settle one final matter with that Big Fisherman before he handed over to him the future leadership of the Apostles. He had a question Peter was to answer with no "hemming" or "hawing." When they got out of earshot of the rest of the disciples, turning to Peter and looking into his face, eye to eye, Jesus put it to him simply:

"Simon, son of John, do you love me?" (JOHN 21:15 ff)

Note that he did not ask Peter, who had been closer to him than any of the others, standing right at his elbow while miracle after miracle was performed, sermon after sermon was preached, lesson after lesson was taught, if even he *understood* him! Nor did he ask Peter if he could *explain* or *define* him! All he asked Simon was if he *loved* him. For if he had a "Yes" to that question, then he had Peter's *heart* and if he had Peter's heart—everything else that Peter had would be his as well.

"Do you love me?" is the same question Jesus puts to us all, eventually. He bides his time until the right moment arrives, as it did with Simon, and when it comes he locks his eyes into ours and *asks*———waiting for a reply.

For those who say "Yes" he reaches out and takes them by the hand, as Albert Schweitzer wrote:

"As of old, by the lakeside, he came to *those* men. . . . He will speak to us the same words, 'Follow me' . . . and set us to the tasks which he has to fulfill for our time. He will command. And to those who obey him, whether they be wise or simple, he will reveal himself in the toils, the conflicts, the suffering which they shall pass through in his fellowship, and, as an ineffable mystery they shall learn in their *own experience* . . . who he is."[1]

---

[1] A. Schweitzer, *Quest for the Historical Jesus.*

I Believe in The Holy Spirit

"These things I have spoken to you, while I am still with you. But the Counselor, the Holy Spirit, whom the Father will send in my name, he will teach you all things, and bring to your remembrance all that I have said to you. Peace I leave with you; my peace I give to you; not as the world gives do I give to you. Let not your hearts be troubled, neither let them be afraid. You heard me say to you, 'I go away, and I will come to you.' If you loved me, you would have rejoiced, because I go to the Father; for the Father is greater than I. And now I have told you before it takes place, so that when it does take place, you may believe. I will no longer talk much with you, for the ruler of this world is coming. He has no power over me; but I do as the Father has commanded me so that the world may know that I love the Father. Rise, let us go hence." (JOHN 14:25–31)

For many Christians the Holy Spirit is the forgotten member of the Trinity! Less is said and understood about him than any other person of the Godhead. Ask most believers about God as Father or Christ as Son and they can give you some sort of answer. Quiz them about God as Spirit and as often as not you will draw a blank!

Even though he is tough for us to explain, the Spirit is closer to us than anyone else can be. He is God as he has taken up permanent residence in the world and in our lives. He establishes contact with every one of us when we draw our first breath, and he carries us through the rest of our existence, going on with us into eternity. Where God the Father created us, and God the Son poured out his life to save us, it is the Holy Spirit who works *with* and *in* us to keep us whole and moving in the paths of life in which we ought to go. In carrying out his purpose, he has five basic tasks to perform. He *calls, gathers, refashions, enlightens* and *comforts* those who are willing to give him the chance.

His Greek name, *Paraclete,* lines out for us the first of his tasks. The root meaning of that word is "advocate" or "intercessor." In ancient law courts, the *advocate* was a legal expert who had been hired or appointed to plead a person's case before the court. Applied to the Holy Spirit, it describes him as he is at work in our lives. He has a task that moves him in *two directions at once!*

He is sent from eternity to deliver a Divine "calling card" to us, telling us to remember that we are not alone in the universe. As such a messenger with good news, he often is drawn in art and symbols in the shape of a white dove, a sort of heavenly "carrier pigeon" flying straight toward us to deliver a personalized "love note."

His second side of that task is to hold up before us those things we do that bring pain and destruction to ourselves, others and God. When we bend our lives into sinful shapes, he tugs at us to straighten them out. He usually gets started on that venture by gnawing away at the strings of our conscience. He often brings back to life in our minds the deceptive and dishonorable things we've done. He opens our moral closets that we have kept locked and drags out the skeletons we have hidden behind the doors! These he parades back and forth across the stage of our head and heart, making us feel guilty.

He doesn't do that out of a sense of enjoyment at causing us mental anguish. It is a labor he finds painful but necessary to show us how far off course we have gotten and what a dangerous state into which we have put ourselves. Like a lot of our pain it has the useful purpose of informing us that something serious is wrong within us. And what is out of kilter where he is concerned can only be turned around once we *admit* that the *condition exists!* Like the prophet Nathan standing before David, the Spirit points the finger at *us* and says,

"You are the man." (II SAMUEL 12:7)

Once he awakens within us the sense of what needs reshaped in our attitudes or actions, he lays out the means for changing the situation. To get us up off of the floor and get us moving in the right direction, he holds up in front of us the picture of a *loving God* who is willing and ready to forgive us, a God who is *pulling* us toward a more thrilling life rather than waiting for a chance to *clobber* us for our *failures* in the past! As the *advocate* he is the *"pleader,"* who forever seems to be pushing and needling and jabbing us to follow his leading. And like a good *Paraclete* he will not rest his case until he wins.

In addition to *advocate, Paraclete* has another connotation. It describes a person who is sent on a mission *to gather people together.* In this task, the Spirit looks like an old *towncrier* walking through the streets singing out at the top of his voice that all the people within earshot are to follow him to his destination. As God in our midst, he calls out to willing members of humanity, gathering those who respond into an army of faithful pilgrims. These he leads into the mass of the people of God we call the *Church.*

That army of the gathered is not a society of super-clean or perfect people! It is an enormous family of bent-out-of-shape people whose lives have been soiled by their sins. They are persons who have come at the urging of the Spirit from every nook and cranny of the world and out of every age in history. Within the family are people who once may have been corrupt beyond imagination, but who have been able and willing to recognize and admit that fact. The church never has been, in its true form, a *club for the self-styled right-*

eous who really are only the same kind of bent-out-of-shape people but who are too stiff-necked and arrogant to own up to that fact!

But though he leads us *into* the Church in the battered shape in which he finds us, don't be fooled into thinking that the Holy Spirit is going to be *contented to keep us as we are!* Like a skillful carpenter taking over a ramshackle house he has wonderful plans for making a *lot of changes.* As soon as he gets his deed to the property he always sets to work with enthusiasm. Before long, he starts knocking us around in a way we never expected! As C. S. Lewis suggests, perhaps we can understand a *little* of what he has in mind:

> "He's getting the drains right and stopping the leaks in the roof and so on: you know that these jobs needed doing so you are not surprised. But presently he starts knocking the house about in a way that hurts abominably and which doesn't seem to make sense. What on earth is he up to? The explanation is that he is building quite a different house from the one *you* thought of—throwing out a new wing here, putting on an extra floor there, running up towers, making courtyards. You thought you were going to be made into a *decent little cottage:* but he is building a *palace.*"[1]

Being God, the Spirit simply is not satisfied in settling for anything less than the best! Though he is willing to *start* with us *as we are,* he refuses to let us *stay like that.* Once he gathers us together with others like ourselves, he expects changes to take place. He will not lay down the divine tools, nor set aside his plans, until the last board is nailed down and we have been remodeled into the *kind of persons he knows we can be!*

And even *then* he is not content to be our Caller, Gatherer and Architect. The Holy Spirit is determined to be our Teacher as well. After he has completed his overhaul he fully intends to educate us, too. Given the resistance of his student, he knows that he has a life-long job on his hands!

[1] C.S. Lewis. *Beyond Personality.* (N.Y.: Macmillan) p. 49

That is why as long as our hearts beat, the Holy Spirit keeps his hands upon our shoulders. It also explains why he uses every moment and every technique at his disposal to get his points across. He speaks to us through every conceivable avenue to broaden our understanding of God and life, and deepen our faith. Despite our slowness to catch on at times, he never gives up or turns sour on us. What can discourage him, however, is the willful plugging up of our ears. For unless we pay attention, even *God* is at a loss to get through to and communicate with us, I think.

George Bernard Shaw's play, *"Saint Joan,"* holds up that truth. In one of its great scenes, Joan of Arc, the peasant maid of Orlean, is telling the obtuse King Charles about the Heavenly Voices she has heard. All she gets for her efforts is a scoff from the monarch who refuses to believe in her mystic source of understanding:

> "Oh, your voices, your voices! Why don't the voices come to me? I am king, not you," rants Charles.

> "They *do* come to you," replies Joan, "but you do not hear them. You have not sat in the field in the evening listening for them. When the angelus rings, you cross yourself and have done with it; but if you prayed from your heart and listened to the trilling of the bells in the air after they stop ringing, you would hear the voices as well as I."

Is heaven silent for some of us because we do not "pray from the heart" and listen for the Voice? What we hear of the call of God depends to a large extent upon the times and ways we listen. What we catch of the heavenly vision is conditioned by how often we wait at the mount of vision. We understand the eternal truth not merely by *our* efforts to wrap our *minds* around life's problems and puzzles, but when, like the great prophet Habakkuk, we mount to the high tower "to see what God will say to (us)." (HABAKKUK 2:1)

Even though he is Divine, the Holy Spirit can communicate only with such *willing* listeners. He can try for all he is worth to open our eyes and move us and still meet with utter failure. If at the instant he is speaking to us we are preoccupied with lesser things, his approach to us may be lost, and that much of our understanding of life and God may be darkened forever.

The final work of the Holy Spirit is to act as a Comforter for us. True to Jesus' promise, God the Father did not leave us comfortless in this world. When Jesus returned to the heavenly throne he left when he came to earth to live, to love, teach and die for us, the Holy Spirit rushed in to fill the void Jesus' departure created for the early disciples and could create for us. Since that time his presence has continually been a source of strength for the children of God. He has been the Power that has enabled bruised and battered people to stay afloat when life has threatened to overwhelm them. And that has happened because as they took on one problem after another they knew that not only were other *human beings* near enough to help them, but that above all *God, too, was there* at their side, as all sorts of people from beggars to rulers have learned in their turn.

The story has been told of how when the day arrived for Abraham Lincoln to leave Springfield, Illinois for Washington, some friends gathered to send him off, among whom was an elderly Quaker woman. As the others left the President-elect on the rear platform of the train, the little lady took him by the hand and pulled his head down to hers. "Friend Abraham," she whispered in his ear, "God surely will go with thee. Even in thy mansion with all its rooms, his footsteps will be beside thine." Years later, when the raging Civil War tormented him, and his son died and Mrs. Lincoln nearly lost her sanity, those words, whispered on the platform when his journey to the Presidency began, helped carry that great man through. After his assassination, those parting words were found on a small sheet of paper laid in the drawer of the desk at which Lincoln sat when he wrote his letters of consolation to the parents of the Union soldiers lost in battle.

That is the way it always has been for those who have *felt* God's hand in theirs when life has become painful and threatening. As Elton Trueblood has written, for God to *matter* to us he must be *met*, not just *discussed* and *argued* about. And one of the places where he met God was in the fertile fields of the 23rd Psalm. And he tells us in his treatment of that Psalm how that encounter usually takes place:

> "*First* in this psalm God is *spoken* about: 'He maketh me lie down in green pastures.' But in the fourth verse the mood changes: 'Yea, though I walk through the valley of the shadow of death, I will fear no evil; *for thou art with me.*' What it means is that at the profoundest depths men talk not *about* God but *with* him."[2]

And Trueblood is right! Of course he is! The presence of God's Spirit has made saints of beggars and heroes of cowards. He has filled hearts with faith and assurance when it seemed time to abandon all hope. He has buoyed-up people over a life of suffering and given others strength to bear defeat. And he has touched with sympathy and the deepest compassion hearts that otherwise would have been broken with grief.

In every way, the Holy Spirit has been the power of God in time of need. And he has proven himself to be more than sufficient to meet whatever occasion has arisen. He still is a source of inspiration ready to be tapped by whomever is willing to trust him. All he asks is a heart that is willing to throw open its gates and let him in.

[2] E. Trueblood. *The New Man for Our Time.* (N.Y.: Harper and Row) p. 121

I Believe...in The holy catholic Church

"Meanwhile the disciples besought him, saying, 'Rabbi, eat.' But he said to them, 'I have food to eat of which you do not know.' So the disciples said to one another, 'Has anyone brought him food?' Jesus said to them, 'My food is to do the will of him who sent me, and to accomplish his work. Do you not say, There are yet four months, and then comes the harvest? I tell you, lift up your eyes and see how the fields are already white for harvest." (JOHN 4:31–35)

How is your logapedics? Or rather how are you in logapedics? You have never heard the word? Well neither have lots of other people who are vitally involved with what logapedics is all about!

Though it sounds like a disease, the term doesn't have anything to do with any physical illnesses we might have. Logapedics, simply put, is the art of teaching people to speak properly. It has to do with the formation of words and the act of giving them birth. Because it does *that,* it has a key role in helping us to enable other people to know what we have on our minds when we try to communicate with them.

In this series on the Apostles' Creed, we have been working on the logapedics of faith. What draws our attention here is the shape and meaning of the words we profess when we declare:

> "I believe . . . in the holy catholic (or as some persons prefer, 'Christian') Church, the communion of saints."

For all of its brevity, this short affirmation of faith is a real block-buster! It is so stuffed with meaning and challenge that a lifetime of study and wrestling with it cannot wring it dry!

When we say these words, we are telling anyone in the world who is listening and reminding *each other,* that the organism we call the "church" is a God-gathered throng of people who in many ways are so "strange" that they stand out like a sore thumb, or ought to, from the people who live around them. The "church" as the Creed and the Scriptures understand it, is not comprised of buildings, no matter how beautifully stacked their bricks or stone are, or how lovely arranged their glass and art. The "church" is human beings God has scooped up across the ages from every race and nation and washed off in baptism, branding them forever as his own. And his purpose in doing that has been to use them as his hands, feet and mouth, to reach out into the mass of passing people and enlarge their number.

It is tragic that the name *"church"* ever was applied to the *meeting houses* where these God-gathered people have assembled! Such language makes the "church" seem static and fixed and cold and often out-of-date and forbidding to those who stand outside of the doors of such structures!

If you look to the Bible for the clues it gives us to help describe and find the *"church,"* you get to see *what* and *who* it is, in a startlingly different light. There the term we render in English as "church" is the Greek word *ekklesia.* It is a word formed from two Greek stems, *ek* meaning "out from" or "away from" and *klesis,* meaning "an invitation to a place or a position." Together they describe a peculiar bunch of people, invited by God to come to him *out of the crowd* to stand with him for a moment, then go out with him *into that crowd* from which they came to help him love and bind up the wounds we find there.

Don't let the fact that the "called out" are labeled "holy" fool you. That is no claim to our being *better* or *above the crowd* or being set on a *pedestal* from which to look down on the rest! *Hagios,* "holy," means "set apart for divine *use*" not for divine *privilege*. That, I suspect, has made a lot of the "holy" ones a bit uneasy from time to time when they got to understand its implications!

One of the problems with our logapedics, where the word "church" has been involved, is that too many of us have gotten fouled up by thinking that being called by God into his church means that the primary purpose for our lives from that time forward is to spend ourselves getting deeply introspective, treating our existence as though God's invitation to us is a strictly personal, spiritual matter. For broad segments of the church that has been thought to be the chief end of the Christian life! And so the stress frequently has been placed on what prayer, worship and living the faith is to do for *us*. How we are to engage in those things, why we fail to get from them what we expect, often have become the focal points of our gatherings. The church, with *heads bowed* and *hands folded,* has been their picture of the proper Christian posture. And those things have, and always have had, their places, I strongly affirm. But too often such a picture of the church has led it to *stop* with that position, making us believe that Christianity *is* simply a personal, private, spiritual, "what's in it for me" matter . . . which according to the *Creed* and the *Word of God* it is not!

Christianity is not merely a *private, personal* and principally *"spiritual"* affair at all. Christianity is *life lived in community*. It does have personal aspects to it, certainly it does. But being gathered by God to be part of his *peculiar people* at its heart is more concerned with us and our neighbors than it is with us as spiritual, private entities!

Being members of the church *does* begin with God and us as *individuals*. That tug of God that pulls us close enough for him to pick us up, pour water over us and call us *his* by our *names,* has that perpendicular dimension to it, a sort of two-way, God-to-us, link-up. In that sense it is like Bill Cosby says it in his monologue about Noah: "It's you and me Lord, right? It's you and me!" God uses that link-up to get through to our awareness when he is able to do so, so that we can know he *exists,* that we have *to do with him,* that we are *accountable* to him, that we are *loved* by him, and that the single most important aspect of existence is to live our lives in light of him. That is where it all *begins,* with us as individuals he has called to be his church.

But for too many people that is where it all *ends,* too. What some of us miss too often is that there is a second link-up that is involved for God's peculiar people. That is the *horizontal* one that ties persons to persons! We need to remember that we are gathered by God to be his people in relationships with other human beings! Our basic mission is to live life in community with them so that God is able, through us, using us as partners, to save his world and those who live in it! And it is *this* dimension, which too much focus on us as "spiritual" *individuals* has made us forget. We easily become so concerned with *our* well-being and salvation that we focus so strongly on what we have been *saved from,* that we forget what we are *saved for.* We become so concerned about escaping from the "rot of the world" that we forget that the crucial issue for God is *where in the world* we are to invest our lives for him as his people! We get to thinking that we are gathered to live as Christians all by ourselves, in isolation from the rest of the world, with its troubles, temptations and needs.

Repeatedly God has had to shake up his church and bring it back to its senses. Time after time, he has come to remind us, that his purpose for singling us out and rallying us to his service is to share with us the privilege of helping him rescue other human beings from tragedy, as we, with him, plunge into the fields of the world filled with writhing human beings and get *involved there* with helping them in *every sphere* of their *existence.*

The individualistic "religion is a spiritual affair" stuff frequently has tended to hamstring our mission to the *whole* person in a *real world!* It has led too many of us too often to sit in churches, Sunday schools, religious meetings and conference halls, sucking our spiritual thumbs, while the world has been groaning at our doors. It has been one of the prime movers for those who like to divide the world into "religious" and "secular," "spiritual" and "material" spheres, and when that has been pulled off, lead people to believe that the "spiritual" and "religious" have little to do with the "secular" and "material!" Then, you see, Christianity and the church, can be separated neatly from our activities in the "world" where we really live! The word God, then has only to do with these *isolated segments of our lives.*

For all of the upheaval and cracking of outworn attitudes, it is nothing short of astonishing, that we are still being told by some who wish to disengage from the pressing social issues of our day, that the *single concern* of the church is to be with the "souls of people," that "inner dimension," so to speak, and that we ought to leave labor laws, civil rights and child care practices alone. The proper business of the church is to conduct strawberry festivals, quilting bees and rummage sales, but keep its nose and members out of social reform, issues of war and peace and the need for justice and fair opportunity for the down-and-outers of the world! The church, as they would have it, is to talk of the *next world,* tell people about what awaits them *after* they die, teach them about the virtues of suffering unjustly. But the *gutsy* issues of the world, *that* is the work of social workers and "do-gooders!" For such people, *salvation* has to do only with what happens to a person after the embalmer gets to us. It is *not* concerned with the grinding suffering of humankind!

But such a stance runs headlong into the Gospel, the "good news," in the *broad dimensions* God gives it in the mouth of Isaiah the Prophet, when the Lord has him declare that he has been sent by God to:

> "Bring good tidings to the *afflicted,* to *bind up* the *broken hearted,* to *proclaim liberty* to the *captives,* and the *opening of the eyes* of those who are *blind."* (ISAIAH 61:1, ff)

All of which are very *earthy* and *concrete* here-and-now things to be done! For *Salvation,* as you see it here, has to do with the *stuff of life, all* of life, *this* life as well as the *next* one. And there is no area of life into which we, as members of the church, should not stick our noses, then our fingers, then finally our whole beings!

This should be especially clear to Lutherans! It was Luther, you remember, who attacked the idea of monasticism in the Middle Ages. He bombed the monks for acting as though one could be a Christian without working to right the evils of the world. "A monk in a cell is no better than a man in hiding," he said. "The place for God's roses is out among the thorns," he said. "We are not called by God to save ourselves. That, Christ has already done for us," he said. We are to help Christ save the world in every area of its activity. We are sent, as his Church, to reach the *whole person* in the *whole world,* wherever in the world we see such need.

Jesus himself set the pattern for our mission and ministry when he rolled the spiritual and material elements of life into one ball of wax! Jesus took time off after his baptism to go apart for a spiritual retreat and get a fix on his mission as Messiah. For 40 days, he prayed and struggled to see how he was to use his life for human beings. *Immediately,* after coming back from the retreat, he rounded up his disciples for a mission of *healing* as well as *preaching.*

There was the day Jesus lit out for the hills on the other side of the Sea of Galilee. He wanted to worship and get recharged. But when more than 5000 people followed and were fainting from hunger, Christ turned not to give them a "spiritual" lecture on the benefits of fasting! He got down to the "earthy" business of *providing bread and fish to fill their gnawing stomachs!*

For Jesus, discipleship was not a call to center one's attention simply on *oneself.* Nor was it just a nice relationship with *friends* that could settle down into a cozy *introspective fellowship.* It was not a *retreat from life* where one dreamed dreams of the hereafter and ignored the crises of people here and now. It was a *driving, moving love* that sent him *into the world,* to care for and serve, to give and die for it if need be, as the need proved to be. So it is not surprising that he turned the heads of those he gathered around him and taught and marked as his own, in the same direction. And he is still doing the same today. "My food is to *do the will* of him who sent me and *to accomplish his work*," he is saying to us who are now his church . . . "See the fields . . . ready."

Jesus has always hung out the same call for each generation of disciples. For *this* generation, he seems to have written out his call to the church in *neon* and made it blink: "Get involved . . . out there." In *one breath* he was always saying to those who would listen, "Come!" With the *next breath* it was, "Go and give!"

In *one motion* he would pull people out of the crowds and hold them close to him. In the *next motion* he had his hand in the middle of their backs pushing them out into the crowds again, onto the streets and into the fields of the world, where the wounded and needy are to be found. All of which blasts that, "Let's escape from the world," "Let's not get involved," "Religion is a sheer self-improvement project" canard right out of the water.

"*Follow me*, my church, my 'strange' gathered ones," he calls to us. And our answer to that call always will be made not with our *mouths* but with our *feet*. As Frederick Buechner has observed:

> "We always answer with our *feet*. We get up and start following. Or we do not. Maybe we just plant our feet squarely in the ground and pretend we did not hear. Or . . . we move them, but in another direction."[1]

But when we do decide to follow we follow with our feet. And that may lead us into libraries or slums, or hospitals, or law courts, or nurseries, or churches, or wherever it may be that each of us hears that Voice most clearly. And no one but *you* will know *specifically*, where Christ will call *you* to follow and serve with him. Just be certain of this, the world and its people have needs, and as the church, the strange gathered ones, we will be called by Christ to respond to them!

[1] F. Buechner, *The Magnificent Defeat*, pp. 97–98.

And that is what makes being part of the church "catholic," the church found around the world and across the centuries, such a *tough* and *demanding* venture. It is tough because it demands that we put in the center of our lives *God* and *his will* and *his people,* rather than *ourselves* and our *personal desires* and *prejudices* and *ambitions.* And that transition always hurts, because it involves turning our gaze and attention *outward* toward the knotty, thorny and often staggering realities of life, rather than *upward* upon thoughts of clouds to ride upon, and harps to pluck and days of leisure and ease to come!

To get us ready for service in those fields, Christ has gathered us together to *bathe* us with the *water of baptism, feed* us with his *Word* and *reach out* to touch and carry us along by giving us himself to us wearing the *clothes of bread and wine.* But he will never be satisfied to let us *camp in spiritual boxes and dream.* Always he will come to us and will *push* and *probe* and *goad* us to go out of hours and places like that, with all their inspiration and learning and togetherness— to love and sweat, serve and cry over, bind up and worry about "the world and those who dwell therein." (PSALM 24:1b)

Moments of prayer and meditation and study all have their places, certainly they do. We need them. We need each other. But they must always be filling stations for action, not parking places for retirement. For the fields of the world are ready and waiting for your hands and mine! And as we, the *strange, gathered ones* called the *church,* realize that, and act on that, the great, good heart of God is made glad!

I Believe in the Forgiveness of Sins

"As (Jesus) entered Capernaum a centurion came forward to him, beseeching him and saying, 'Lord, my servant is lying paralyzed at home, in terrible distress.' And he said to him, 'I will come and heal him.' But the centurion answered him, 'Lord I am not worthy to have you come under my roof; but only say the word and my servant will be healed. For I am a man under authority, with soldiers under me; and I say to one, 'Go' and he goes, and to another, 'Come' and he comes, and to my slave, 'Do this,' and he does it.' When Jesus heard him he marveled, and said to those who followed him, 'Truly I say to you, not even in Israel have I found such faith. I tell you, many will come from east and west and sit at table with Abraham, Isaac and Jacob in the Kingdom of heaven, while the sons of the kingdom will be thrown into the outer darkness; there men will weep and gnash their teeth.' And to the centurion Jesus said, 'Go; be it done for you as you have believed.' And the servant was healed at that very moment."
(MATTHEW 8:5–13)

If there is any one thing about human beings that the last decade brought home to me with a thud, it is the deep seated feelings of unworthiness that marks so many of us. Though often camouflaged with an outer crust of self sufficiency and cock-suredness inside of themselves scads of people are harboring an aching sense of guilt.

Haunted by skeletons in their moral closets that they cannot handle any more, I have come to meet them as they have walked into my life in various degrees of misery. What I see as I look into their faces are drained-out persons who have been dragging through life under the burden of the heavy blanket of self-disgust and gloom.

Their number is astonishing when all around them sermons are being preached and written, books are pouring out and even talk shows are centering on the subject of living as freed-up people who should be able to leap-frog failures of the past. Together, one should imagine, they should all add up to the power to lift any burden from a person's conscience.

And yet the line of people with up-tight lives and empty eyes, is *growing* instead of *shrinking*. On they come with sagging shoulders and fractured relationships, and often with emotion-caused illnesses, all brought on by the weight of misused yesterdays which they still carry on their backs.

That the line did not just begin to form in the last decade, the Apostles' Creed makes abundantly clear. In the handful of truths about God and life it holds up for the world to see and come to terms with, sin and failure, and the treatment for both, receive clear and powerful attention. In just seven words the dilemma that can wear us out is addressed without fudging or varnish. It is all set out clearly and simply—

"I believe in . . . the forgiveness of sins."

Most of the times when I have heard teachers or preachers expound on that declaration, the sole emphasis has been placed on the willingness of God to clear our pasts of the trash we have accumulated there. The point is rightly made, and needs to be made regularly and repeatedly, that the chance for a new tomorrow, in spite of the shambles we have made of our yesterdays, comes as a magnificent *gift* from God. You and I can in no way wipe out our sins ourselves or call back time to rework them. It is only the strong hand of God that can lift the weight from our lives that failure after failure has piled upon us.

For Edward Fitzgerald was right when he wrote:

> "The moving finger writes, and having writ moves on: *nor* all your piety nor wit shall lure it back to cancel half a line nor all your tears wash out a word of it."

St. Paul was also right when he told the church at Corinth:

> "For by *grace* you have been saved through faith; . . . it is the *gift* of God." (EPHESIANS 2:8)

That word "grace" is the Greek term *charis*. It describes some one coming to another to bring a gift, or to provide care, or to help to lift a burden. It is always something done without a fee or repayment in mind. It is an act lived out that cannot be bought or earned at any price. It is an accurate description of the *labor of love* forgiveness actually is. God, without bribes, steps along side of each of us, and puts out his hand to cut the cords that bind our sins to our bent backs. The awesomeness of that act can never be recalled too much.

What often is *glossed over* and mentioned *too little,* however, is the fact that for all of the willingness and eagerness of God to hoist that burden of the past, his efforts too often go for nothing, because many times we will not let him give us the gift he comes to bring! He stretches out his hand with the divine knife to cut our past loose and we push him off, and back away and go on carrying the load, as incredible as that all sounds!

And it is precisely here, I have come to learn, that the real problem in the chain of forgiveness is to be found. While most of us believe in the forgiveness of sins as a *theoretical* power or activity of God, especially for *others,* many of us, perhaps *most* of us, have trouble at times believing in the forgiveness of sins for *ourselves!* For a wide variety of reasons, accepting forgiveness, really and truly *believing* that God is eager and willing to do that for us, is one of the most difficult parts of the Christian faith with which we have to deal.

Perhaps the thing that causes most of the trouble is believing that *God* is willing to forgive and deal so lovingly with us, when so many of the experiences we have had with *human beings* have told us that such things can never be true. So much of what we believe about *God* is based on what we learn about life from other *people*. God seems to be just a blown-up version of the significant persons in our lives.

Marc Connelly, in his play "The Green Pastures," shows how it works. In one scene from that play the little children gathering at Sunday School try to imagine how heaven will look when they finally get there. They finally decide that it will be a gigantic *fish fry* going on up above the clouds, as the great days of joy were on the plantation where they lived. They also are convinced that the God who will be hosting the affair will bear a striking resemblance to Mr. De Shay, who just happened to be their beloved pastor.

That is not surprising. How else do you learn of someone you have *not seen* unless you have some clues from people you *do know?* Parents, particularly, help shape not only our attitudes toward *life,* but often sow the seeds for our understanding of how *God must act,* as well.

I know that where forgiveness is concerned my father had a powerful influence on me. He was a man who for all his positive contributions to my life made forgiveness something it took me nearly half my life to accept. Ours was a home that was ruled by a law that never bent. Every mistake that was made had to be paid for in full. Even if the punishment was stored up for a day of reckoning somewhere down the line, the time always came when the bill came due, and on *judgment day* there were *no discounts!*

Sometimes the price for "sins" seemed high. Like the time when in the spring of the year I violated the commandment that said, "At 5:00 p.m. sharp every child in the house has to be seated at the dinner table, washed, hair combed, dressed in fresh clean clothes waiting for his mother to put down the food for supper!" It happened on the first good day after the snows had melted, and the sun had come out to dry out the empty lot at the end of our block. I was on the way home from school when I saw that some friends of mine had started a stickball game, and had saved a place for me. Putting down my books I got into the spirit of things and lost track of the time. All of a sudden one of my friends, who knew the "law" as well as I did, said, "Frank, it's 5 minutes after 5! You had better fly!"

If you ever wanted to see a little boy fly you should have been there that day! I shot down the street and up the stairs to the second floor of the house where we lived and bolted into the kitchen. Guess who was standing there waiting for me to arrive! And the price for my sins? . . . Six weeks in the house, every day after school till bed time, all day Saturday and Sunday. Six *weeks* for 5 *minutes* . . . just when the snows were giving way to spring.

What I learned in a home like that was that *that* must be how life really is everywhere! All things must be *paid for,* nothing is a *gift* or *written off,* even where God is concerned. And those assumptions, branded into us early, continue to operate within us even though we *think we have forgotten* or *gotten over* them. And I have found that they create some of the highest barriers we must hurdle where forgiveness is concerned.

A lot of the people with whom I deal are struggling with the same problem. Little or no love has been shown to them by *those who were closest to them.* When you talk of *God* as a *forgiving heavenly Father* the image itself can become the problem. How can *any* father be forgiving when the only father you have known has been faithless, miserable, a drunk or one who battered and abused you before he abandoned you and made you take on life alone?

You see what *we* do as people and to each other has enormous power to affect the deepest levels of our lives. Some are bruised to the point where they have a hard time trusting God *as he is,* because of the distorted picture of him they have been given by earthlings. So, while it is possible to say we "believe in the forgiveness of sins,"

57

with the words still ringing in our ears we walk on with those sins still on our backs because the forgiveness of which we spoke must have been meant for *anyone* but *us!*

Another thing that makes it hard for *God's* forgiveness to set us free is our *pride*. As human beings we seem to come equipped with, or soon develop, our own credo that says, "I would rather do it *myself,* thank you!" Something seems to ooze from our bones that tells us that to *need anybody,* even God, to supply something we lack is to fall short of our ideal, the self-sufficient, self-made man or woman, who is indebted to no one. George Bernard Shaw stated it for many when speaking on the subject, he said:

"Forgiveness is a beggar's refuge. We must pay our debts."

Like a tottering child, we push away the supporting hands shouting, "I can make it *alone.*"

What I have found is that with most such people, this problem in accepting forgiveness is a cover-up for something else. Scratch the *pride* that is on the surface and underneath you may find that the *arrogance* is just a thin coating hiding *inferiority.* Our bluster is a cover-up for the fear of rejection. It is our security blanket against counting on someone's promise that won't hold up when we bank on it. We don't *matter enough* for it to be *true!* It is like Charlie Brown when Lucy keeps goading him to boot the football she is holding up for him on the kicking tee. Though he wants to believe that *this time* she will not pull it away just when he is ready to put his foot into it, when she does, and he falls flat on his back, he sighs in resignation, "That's what a nothing like me deserves, I guess."

One of the defense mechanisms we use to hold on to our blankets of security is never to trust the promise of anyone *who values us more than we do.* We rationalize our attitudes by saying that everybody knows that what *we* think of ourselves is so! So we act like Linus in another of the "Peanuts" strips Charles Schulz has drawn. Only this time Charlie is chiding Linus for turning his back on his friends for fear that they will not choose him for a pick-up game of baseball:

"What if *everyone* was like you? What if we *all* tried to hide our feelings of inferiority by saying we don't want to play. Huh? What then?" says Charlie. "What if everyone in the *whole world* suddenly decided to *run away* from that problem like you?" Linus, clutching his blanket more securely than ever, puts his little nose up in the air and replies: "Well, if they did, *we would all be running in the same direction.*"

Often we *do* run in the *same direction* where inferiority and insecurity are concerned. It is astonishing how many people really *hate* themselves. They are constantly beating themselves down, and criticizing themselves as failures, and they have long catalogues of faults supporting their self-evaluation. What is surprising is that they usually are people *others think* have a bundle of things going for them. They are the kind of persons we would like to call friends, or who supply strength and warmth to others. But somehow the tote boards most of us carry inside ourselves, that record our self-impressions, seem always to short out on the *plus* side and register only the *negative!* Why this is so I have yet to fully understand. That it *is* so, all the farther most of us have to walk for proof is to the nearest mirror and look in.

If the second article of the Apostles' Creed and the Old and New Testaments show anything, it is that *God is willing to forgive* us when we are at the bottom of the gutter. Our own constant self-battering can lead us to believe that he is no more willing to accept us than we are. So that when he comes to do just that it makes us deaf to his offer.

One day a man who was battling that same problem was in the crowd that surrounded Jesus as he was entering Capernaum. A Roman centurion, whose servant had fallen ill, had gotten so frantic in an effort to help him recover that he went looking for the Carpenter. One of the hated conquerors, he must have scoured everywhere for a cure before he turned to the Galilean. He had a whole string of things against him which he *knew* would get him turned down should he even get to see Jesus. It was his countrymen who had taken the freedom of Jesus' people away. They had defiled the temple of the God the Teacher he sought claimed was his Father.

He was not even a Jew, but had his own string of deities for whose help he had asked in the past. He had every reason to think his plea for help would get short shrift when it was made.

But when all else had failed, the centurion came to Jesus for help, and you can almost hear the quiver in his voice when he lays out his plea:

> "Lord, my servant is lying paralyzed at home, in terrible distress." (MATTHEW 8:6)

And he is nearly *floored* when Jesus' immediate response is:

> "I will come and heal him." (MATTHEW 8:7)

The centurion was *true to character,* when *after the request* he makes *was granted,* he pours out to Jesus the reasons Christ *should not come to his house* to do the healing. Christ is *equally true to the character of God* when he shows that when the door is unlocked for him to do so he is willing to come to *any of us* to put us back together again!

And that is true where *forgiveness* is the gift needed for wholeness. But there can be none of it for those of us who need forgiveness, if we choose to tie Jesus' hands and refuse to accept it when he holds it out. For in a real way the power of forgiveness is never automatic. To take effect we must let God do his work of setting us free on *his terms,* not ours. He longs to lift the burdens of the past from our humped-over backs *freely,* as a *loving gift.* He is eager to restore light to our faces. He nearly begs us with his persistent offer to do both. And it all can be ours if we will *trust him to do what he says he will,* give us a whole new lease on life. *It can happen to us* and *take effect* if we stop running long enough for him to latch on to us.

In a moment that can turn our *grief* into *joy* he can cut from our necks the millstones of guilt we have been dragging around for years. And we can *experience for ourselves* the forgiveness that the Creed *proclaims* and *promises* was meant not just for some *faceless world,* but that was and is held out to *you* and to *me,* too.

I Believe in the Resurrection

"And when the sabbath was past, Mary Magdalene, and Mary the mother of James, and Salome, bought spices, so that they might go and anoint him. And very early on the first day of the week they went to the tomb when the sun had risen. And they were saying to one another, 'Who will roll away the stone for us from the door of the tomb?' And looking up, they saw that the stone was rolled back; for it was very large. And entering the tomb, they saw a young man sitting on the right side, dressed in a white robe; and they were amazed. And he said to them, 'Do not be amazed; you seek Jesus of Nazareth, who was crucified. He has risen, he is not here; see the place where they laid him. But go, tell his disciples and Peter that he is going before you to Galilee; there you will see him, as he told you.' And they went out and fled from the tomb; for trembling and astonishment had come upon them; and they said nothing to any one, for they were afraid." (MARK 16:1–8)

There is no sound that has a more crushing sense of finality about it then the first shoveful of dirt that falls on the lid of a coffin. Its dull thud is the most undeniable piece of evidence, that despite all of our attempts to avoid the reality, the person in the casket is dead. Until then some of the sting of death can be fended off. But once the lid is closed and the casket is lowered into the grave, and the grave is sealed, all pretense ends and we have to admit that that person's life has come to an end, and with it, its labors and ambitions and dreams! In rushes the pain of seeing "finish" written to that earthly existence, and that closing can rock us back on our heels!

The disciples of Jesus were just as shaken as *they* watched the stone rolled against the Master's tomb on Good Friday. As the rock slid into place, and it was sealed, the grave looked dreadfully secure. Choked up with grief, the disciples left the grave site with a dragging, listless gait, beaten and dejected.

A contemporary writer has imagined what it would have been like to talk to a few of the apostles as they shuffled their way home. He pictures himself walking up to the three who had been closest to Jesus to probe their feelings.

> "Why are you so downhearted, Peter?"
> "Jesus is dead," he answers.
> "Well James, why are you so glum?"
> "Jesus is dead."
> "And you, John, what has gone wrong with you? Where is your old spark?"
> "Jesus is dead."

Pressing the conversation he goes a bit farther, inquiring about their plans for the future:

> "Well then, Peter, what are you going to do with your life from now on?"
> "Go back to my boat and start fishing again, I guess."
> "And you, James and John, what is in store for you now that Jesus is dead?"
> "Back to mending nets."

Still loaded with gloom, they trudge on down the road, for all appearances done in. Their dream had exploded and the future they saw held nothing worth speaking of! Three days later, the same reporter meets the *same* men coming down the *same* road. This time they are moving so briskly, and with such springy steps, they seem hardly to touch the ground. Catching up and falling in step he asks them why the change. With one accord the answer comes back:

"Jesus is alive!"

"The only thing imaginary about it all is the form of the conversation," says Dr. Merrill Abbey. "The change is a matter of record." What *started* that change was the startling words of an angel on Easter morning: "You seek Jesus of Nazareth who was crucified. He has risen, he is not here." (MARK 16:6) What clinched the matter, and made it stick, was the fact that the words were proven *true* by the appearance of Christ to these three men who had seen him die on a cross and watched him sealed in his grave. Not only those three men, but a multitude of Jesus' friends, sensible people who knew a secure tomb when they saw one, became equally convinced that Jesus had risen from the dead. And out they went to preach the message that was to turn the history of the world and individual lives in a new direction.

After twenty centuries of fierce scrutiny, what happened on Easter is still the heart of the Christian message. And it is a declaration packed with power! "I believe," declares the church, that "the third day (Jesus) rose from the dead," and because he rose, "I believe . . . in the resurrection of the body, and the life everlasting. Amen."

From the day of the first Easter until now, Christians have declared that the Resurrection of Jesus is an *historic fact*. It was not the dream of a few Jewish fishermen, or the figment of their imagination. The Jesus who had been taken from the cross and laid in a borrowed tomb on Friday, was the same Jesus who slipped off his shroud and walked out of that grave alive again Sunday morning.

All the marks of his crucifixion were still present and visible. The nail scars were still in his hands and feet, and the spear wound was still in his side. He was able to speak and be spoken to and could be touched and seen. He sat down to supper and broke bread with his friends. He walked along the lake shore where he often had taught, and waited for his disciples to finish their work so they could gather around him as they had before his death. There was no possibility for anyone else to be mistaken for him! Those who were closest to him during his ministry were absolutely convinced that this Figure beside them was really *Jesus!*

Nor can the resurrection be written off as a *lie,* fabricated by a few disciples to deceive Jesus' enemies. It was the disciples themselves who were the first skeptics when it came to the matter of accepting the resurrection! They wrote off the news as nothing but foolish and irresponsible babbling. When the women returned from the tomb and finally got up the courage to describe what they had seen, the men to whom they spoke disregarded their story as an "idle tale." (LUKE 24:11) Even when Mary Magdalene first saw that the grave was empty, it never entered her mind that Jesus could have come back to life. She was moved to tears because she thought some grave robber had looted the tomb and carted off her Lord! (JOHN 20:15)

No, the resurrection was not a lie made up by the disciples. *They* wouldn't believe it when they were first told of it! But when Jesus himself stood in front of them, and stretched out his hands for their inspection, they not only believed he was alive, but then were willing to die for that certainty, as all but one of them did. The resurrection of Jesus is an *historic fact!*

But the resurrection of Christ was *more* than a mere event in history. It also was a *shaking reality* for more than one person. When Jesus refused to stay dead and walked out of his grave, not even his *colleagues* knew quite what to make of it. They were thrilled, to be sure, but they were frightened at the same time. How would *you* feel if three days after you attended a man's funeral he walked into your kitchen this morning while you were at breakfast? If you are anything like I am you would fall all over yourself looking for the nearest exit!

Jesus' resurrection rattled the disciples, too. Some of the first to learn of the event were shocked into silence. St. Mark records in his Gospel that after the women at the tomb were told that Jesus was alive:

"They went out and fled . . . for trembling and astonishment had come upon them; and they said nothing to anyone, for they were afraid." (MARK 16:8)

Wouldn't you have done the same? Wouldn't you be afraid that those you button-holed to tell what you had experienced would think you had slipped a mental cog?

And there were *others* who were even more stunned by it all. The *authorities* who had put Jesus to death must have nearly dropped their teeth! In the religious court *conniving men* had sentenced Jesus to the cross on the testimony of paid liars. In the barracks *Roman guards* had spit on him and flounted Jesus as a clownish king! On the knob of Calvary the *people* who had watched him being spiked to his bloody perch had poked fun at him, making his last hours more miserable than the nails alone could. When he was carried off to his grave the *religious prigs* thought at last they had him out of their way—and that they could shut up forever their acts against him with the stone door of the tomb.

Just to be safe, you remember, Pilate had that door sealed and posted a guard to prevent anyone from tampering with the body. Every care was taken to fasten down the victory they felt they had won. But though every precaution had been taken to secure the tomb from the *outward tampering of human beings,* there was nothing that Pilate or anyone else could do to ward off the *tampering of God!* After two nights and a day:

"Behold there was a great earthquake; for an angel of the Lord descended from heaven, and came and rolled back the stone, and sat upon it." (MATTHEW 28:2)

I love that phrase "and (he) *sat* upon it." It makes me glow and tingle all over! It supplies the proper finishing touch to the event! After doing his wondrous work, that messenger of God, as if defying the Romans, the crowds, the priests and all the powers of evil to overcome the plans of God, jauntily sat upon the very object the enemies of Jesus thought they could use to shut him in! Not all the legions of Rome, or any other power, is worth a hoot when God makes up his mind to act, then acts!

The stone rolled away! The grave cracked! Jesus threw aside his grave cloth and stood up! And stepping out of the tomb he made a shambles of all the cocky confidence his antagonists had shown three days earlier. He served notice on Easter that it was time for those who stand against him to stop laughing in their beards and start shaking at the knees. He was, and is, back in business and he is back to *stay,* and people everywhere must now reckon with him and that includes not only petty officials like Pilate and Caiaphas, but run of the mill people on the streets all over the world, too.

The resurrection of Jesus is not only a picture covered with Easter lilies and new hats. It is a *day of judgment* when people are forced to make a choice for or against this risen and present Christ. He is not a memory you can write off and forget. He is not a figure cooked up to provide a bustling business for clothing manufacturers and candy makers! He is a living, pulsating, reaching Being, who is *here* in *this place today,* asking us where we stand with him. So, Easter is not all sentiment and anthems! It is a matter of life or death day for us, depending on where we stand. And for those who stand *against* Jesus, his resurrection is a shocking fact, indeed!

But his resurrection is a glorious and comforting fact for those who love and trust him, and claim him as Lord. At no moment is that comfort greater than when we must face death in our own right. Jesus' journey to the grave lighted a lantern in the darkness of the unknown, and its glimmer showed that beyond the tomb there is life anew. However fearsome and yawning the mouth of the grave appears, it has no real teeth to hurt us any more, and no more chains to tie us down forever. Jesus *ripped out both* on Easter morning. When he left it he had swept the grave clean of all threat, and refashioned it into a *resting place* where we stop over on our way to eternity.

Until the break of dawn on the day Jesus arose, such a view of death was only a pipe dream for humanity. Before he killed it, death was the great final act for every human being. Though from the start of time people had hoped that there might be existence after their last breath was spent, eternal life was only a longing, a wistful speculation. But when Jesus stepped out of the shadows into the sunlight of the garden on Easter morning, eternal life was no longer a fantasy; he had made it a reality! So *great* a reality that the early Christians were willing to base their entire faith upon its being true.

> "If there is no resurrection from the dead," Paul wrote to the believers in Corinth, "then Christ has not been raised; If Christ has not been raised, then our preaching is in vain and your faith is in vain. We are found to be misrepresenting God, because we testified of God that he raised Christ whom he did not raise if it is true the dead are not raised . . . and . . . those who have fallen asleep in Christ have perished . . . (and) we of all men are most to be pitied." (I CORINTHIANS 15:12–14)

What Paul said is true! If Jesus *had remained in his tomb* he at best would have been another martyred prophet! Like others before him, people might have sighed over what a shame it had been for him to end his life so early and in so tragic a way. At worst, he would have been branded a visionary and liar, who had led those who gave him their lives to believe he was something he was not. He had promised clearly that he would rise again three days after his death. He had promised his followers that because *he* would live *they* would have life also. He promised a thief dying on a cross next to his that he would take him into paradise with him. If death had ended it all for him none of these promises would have been kept. If he had *not risen* . . . if he had *not* come back to *life . . . if . . .* but he *did!* "On the third day he rose" . . . a Saviour who would not stay dead!

His return pumped new hope and assurance and strength into the lives of Christians everywhere. How great that hope was can be seen in the cemeteries where the early church buried her saints. Side by side with pagans the disciples were laid to rest, but they were worlds apart when it came to the conviction each had about what death had in store for them.

On many of the Roman gravestones were carved seven letters, each one standing for the first word of four short sentences. The initials, "N.F.," "F.," "N.S.," "N.C.," were so well known that they didn't need to be spelled out. "Non fui," "fui," "non sum," "non curo." "I was not," "I was," "I am not," "I do not care." In contrast to them, stood the inscriptions chisled or painted on the vaults of Christians. Not cold resignation to the power of death, they gave bubbling declarations of the confidence they had in the power of God. "Vivit," "He lives!" "Cum Christos," "with Christ." "Accercitus ab Deo," "Called by God!" For death had lost its awful sting for them. Their Master had sprung the lock on its dungeon as he emerged on Easter morning. And they knew it could not hold any of them captive any longer. *Jesus had set them free and they were free indeed!*

That freedom is *ours* as much as it was *theirs!* Though it still is the mysterious road, Jesus' going through the Valley of the Shadow of Death and coming back again has shown us that the way is clear. Because of *that* day we can look death right in the eye and move straight toward it, knowing that death will have to move aside for us. All we need do is follow the trail left by a dragged cross and the foot prints of the One who lugged it—until we look up and see standing in front of us a *risen* Christ, alive, and shining in all his glory!

Notes

Notes

Notes

Notes

Notes

Notes

Notes

Notes

Notes

Notes